D1374335

SHERLOCK HOLMES'

Rudimentary Puzzles

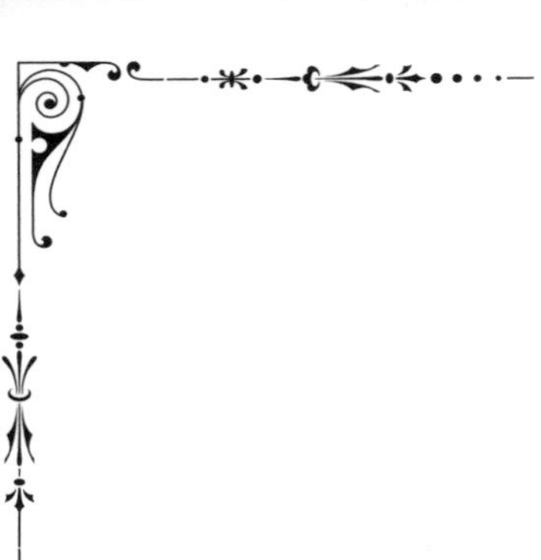

THIS IS A CARLTON BOOK

Published by Carlton Books Ltd
20 Mortimer Street
London W1T 3JW

A CIP catalogue for this book is available from the British Library.

ISBN 978-1-78097-963-2

Text and puzzles: Tim Dedopulos

The publishers would like to thank Mary Evans Picture Library for their kind permission to reproduce the pictures in this book.

Content previously published as *The Sherlock Holmes Puzzle Collection: The Lost Cases.*

Printed in Dubai

SHERLOCK HOLMES'

Rudimentary Puzzles

Riddles, enigmas and challenges inspired by the world's greatest crime-solver

Dr John Watson

Contents

	Question	Answer

STRAIGHTFORWARD

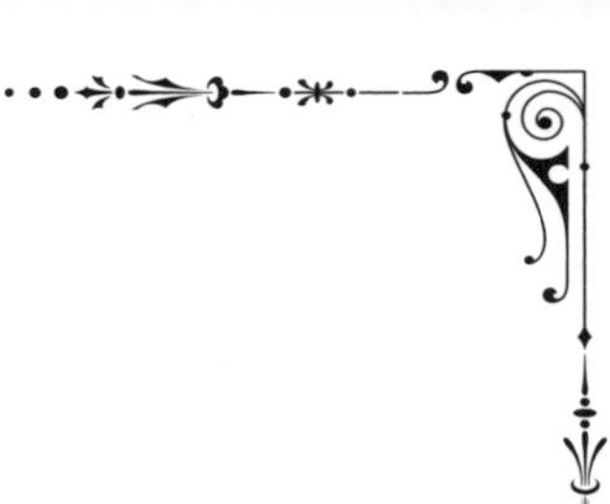

Introduction

The name of my dear friend and companion Mr Sherlock Holmes is familiar to all who possess any interest whatsoever in the field of criminal investigation. Indeed, there are some weeks where it hardly seems possible to pick up a newspaper without seeing his name splashed luridly across the front page. Unlike so many, however, his renown is justly deserved – not for nothing has he frequently been heralded as England's greatest detective, living or dead. Personally, I suspect that his abilities are unmatched anywhere in the world at this time.

I myself have been fortunate enough to share in Holmes' extraordinary adventures, and if I have been unable to rival his insight, I have consoled myself by acting as his de facto chronicler. I also flatter myself a little with the notion that I have, betimes, provided some little warmth of human companionship. We have spent many years, on and off, sharing rooms at 221b Baker Street, and I like to think that the experience has enriched both our existences. My name, though it is of little matter, is John Watson, and I am by profession a doctor.

My dear friend has long had a passionate ambition to improve the minds of humanity. He has often talked about writing a book that will help to instil the habits which he considers so absolutely vital to the art of deduction. Such a tome would be a revolutionary step in the history of mankind, and would most certainly address observation, logical analysis, criminal behaviour, scientific and mathematical knowledge, clear thinking, and much more besides. Alas, it has yet to materialize, for the world is full of villainy, and Sherlock Holmes is ever drawn to the solution of very real problems.

But over the course of our adventures, Holmes has never given up on the cause of improving my modest faculties. On innumerable occasions, he has presented me with opportunities to engage my mind, and solve some problem or other which to him is perfectly clear from the information already available. These trials have sometimes been quite taxing, and have not always come at a welcome moment, but I have engaged in all of them to the very best of my abilities. To do otherwise would be to dishonour the very generous gift my friend is making me in devoting time to my analytical improvement.

In truth, I do believe that his ministrations have indeed helped. I consider myself to be more aware than I was in my youth, and less prone to hasty assessments and faulty conclusions. If I have gained any greater talent in these areas, it is entirely thanks to the efforts that my friend has exerted on my behalf, for it is most certainly not an area for which I am naturally disposed. Give me a sickly patient, and I feel absolutely confident of swiftly arriving at the appropriate diagnosis and, to the limits provided by medical science, of attaining a successful recovery for the

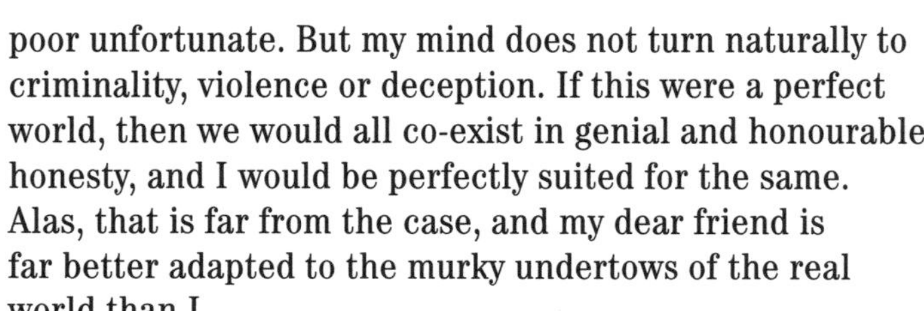

poor unfortunate. But my mind does not turn naturally to criminality, violence or deception. If this were a perfect world, then we would all co-exist in genial and honourable honesty, and I would be perfectly suited for the same. Alas, that is far from the case, and my dear friend is far better adapted to the murky undertows of the real world than I.

Still, as I have already attested, Holmes' little trials have had a beneficial effect even on me. For one who is more readily disposed to such efforts, the results may well be commensurately powerful. Thus, I have taken the liberty of assembling this collection.

Working assiduously from my notes, I have compiled somewhere in the region of seventy of the puzzles that Holmes has set me over the years. I have been assiduous in ensuring that I have described the situation as I first encountered it, with all pertinent information reproduced. The answers are as detailed as I can usefully make them. Some I managed to answer successfully myself; for others, I have reproduced Holmes' explanations as accurately as my notes permit.

To improve the accessibility a little, I have attempted to order the trials into approximate groupings of difficulty – rudimentary and straightforward, to be exact. Holmes has a devious mind, and there were times when he was entirely determined to baffle me, whilst on other occasions, the problems were simple enough to serve as illustrative examples of certain principles. I believe that I have broadly succeeded in classifying the difficulty of his riddles, but I beg your indulgence in so uncertain a matter. Every question is easy, if you know the answer, and the opposite holds equally true.

It is my fervent hope that you will find this little volume enlightening and amusingly diverting. If it may prove to sharpen your deductive sense a little, that would be all the vindication that I could ever possibly wish; all the credit for such improvement would be due Holmes himself. I, as always, am content to be just the scribe. I have made every effort to ensure that the problems are all amenable to fair solution, but if by some remote happenchance that should prove not the case, it must be clear that the blame lies entirely on my shoulders, and that none should devolve to my dear companion.

My friends, it is with very real pleasure that I present to you this volume of the puzzles of Mr Sherlock Holmes.

I remain, as always, your servant,

Dr John H. Watson.

JHWatson

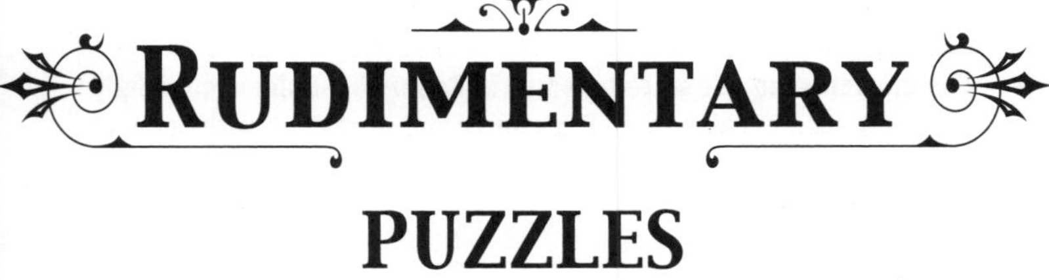

RUDIMENTARY PUZZLES

"Each new discovery furnishes a step which leads on to the complete truth."

Sherlock Holmes

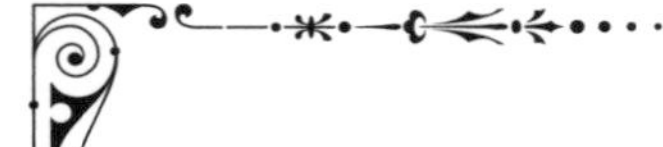

On the Strand

During *The Nasty Affair of the Highwayman's Daughter*, Mr Sherlock Holmes and I found ourselves in a luxurious room on the third floor of a hotel on the Strand. The woman in question – I hesitate to describe her as a lady – was as black-hearted as any I've encountered. We were holed up in Room 303, Holmes cunningly disguised as a Keralan fakir. Our quarry was next door, with some of her next targets. We were preparing to apprehend her when, sadly, events overtook us.

There was a shriek from Room 304, and then a woman's voice shouting, "No, Hugo! Don't shoot! No!" This was followed by a loud gunshot.

We immediately made a dash for 304. The door was unlocked, and we burst in. I'm not ashamed to say that I had my revolver in my hand. Inside, we found a grim scene. The highwayman's daughter lay dead on the floor. At the far end of the room clustered three people, all white-faced, in clear shock. The gun lay at their feet, where it had clearly been dropped by nerveless hands.

Holmes took one look at the group, and said, "Obviously a teacher, a tailor and a lawyer," indicating each in turn. "Watson, restrain the..."

"Lawyer," I said, seizing the unique chance to stick my oar in.

"Clearly," Holmes said, with just the faintest hint of irritation. But how did I of all people know which was the guilty party?

SOLUTION ON PAGE 100

GRANDDAD

You might be interested in this minor follow-up to *The Nasty Affair of the Highwayman's Daughter*. A day later, Holmes and I were back in our lodgings at 221b Baker Street, and I was writing up my notes on the case. Holmes sat there thoughtfully for a period of time, puffing his pipe, whilst I scratched away with my pen.

Eventually, he turned to me. "Her father was quite old, you know," he said.

It seemed an odd point for Holmes to make. "Oh?" I replied.

He nodded. "Older than her grandfather, in fact."

"What?"

He arched an eyebrow at my reaction.

Whatever did he mean?

SOLUTION ON PAGE 100

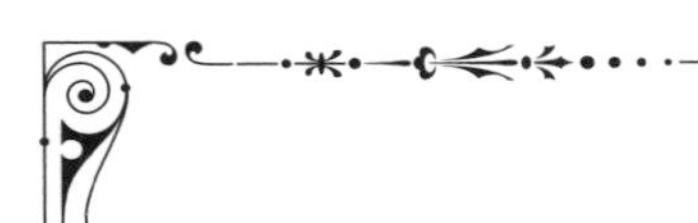

SPHERES

Early on in our relationship, as I have already mentioned elsewhere, Holmes decided that my mental faculties and deductive abilities could be improved by rigorous practice. He took it upon himself to torment me with all manner of conundrums. These were generally presented without warning on the grounds that deduction often had to be called upon under pressure.

I had just sunk into a delightfully hot bath one evening when Holmes' voice floated in to me. "Imagine a ball, Watson."

"Very well," I called back, confident that my quiet sigh had gone unheard.

"Make it a perfect sphere. And don't sigh! Your betterment is the most worthy of causes."

"Indeed," I replied. "So, I have this sphere. What now?"

"Tell me, if you can, what is the probability that any three points chosen at random will fall into a single hemisphere on its surface? You may assume that the dividing line between hemispheres is vanishingly small."

"I shall," I said, and setting relaxation aside, began thinking.

Can you find the solution?

SOLUTION ON PAGE

HOOKLAND

Holmes and I found ourselves in rural Hookland one Tuesday afternoon, some miles east of Coreham, just in sight of Eden Tor. Holmes had taken on the guise of a local farmer, in order to better observe the movements of Major C. L. Nolan. We were standing at a fence, looking over the estates that Nolan was currently visiting, when a genuine local approached us. Holmes turned and leaned back against the fence to watch the newcomer approach, elbows resting behind him on the top strut.

The fellow came to about ten feet away, and stopped.

"Yalreet, boi?" said Holmes conversationally.

"Yalreet," replied the farmer. "Ow's yur mools?"

Holmes scratched his chin thoughtfully. "Li'l buggers is 'ow."

The pair of them continued in this fashion for some time, before the fellow lolloped off again, apparently satisfied as to our bona fides. Once he'd gone, Holmes explained that they'd been talking about moles.

"Our visitor claimed to have caught an entire nest of moles this morning," Holmes told me. "He furthermore suggested that five of them were completely blind in the right eye, four blind in the left, three sighted in the left eye, two sighted in the right, and one sighted in both. I told him the least number of moles that could be, which is when he nodded and left."

"So you weren't discussing Potemkin after all, then?" I muttered.

How many moles did the farmer catch?

SOLUTION ON PAGE 101

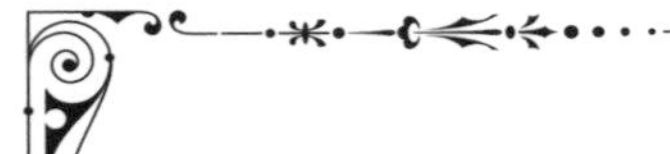

THE WATCHMEN

Holmes and I had cause to observe a warehouse near Wapping Docks during the adventure of the frightened carpenter. A rather expensive necklace had been stolen and we had been charged with its safe return. The warehouse was guarded by a pair of rough-looking men with a little sentry post. Every hour on the hour, one of them would start off on a complex route around the grounds, winding in and out of stacks of pallets at a constant pace, returning finally to the post 45 minutes later.

The men took it in turns to make their round, and the route that they took was always the same, but sometimes they progressed in a clockwise manner, heading left from the hut, and sometimes anticlockwise, heading right. This choice appeared to be settled, as far as we could tell, by the toss of a coin.

"If I were going to assault this place," Holmes said, after some hours of observation, "I know when I'd choose. The guard is in the same spot at a specific time every hour. That's when I'd strike."

"How can you possibly know that?" I protested. "You don't know which way the fellow is going to head."

"It's obvious," Holmes said.

How?

19

SOLUTION ON PAGE

The Prison

"You are incarcerated, Watson," Holmes told me one morning over my kippers.

"I am?"

"Indeed so. In some backwater town in Albania, say."

"How unfortunate," I replied. "Their prison cook seems quite satisfactory, however."

"Luckily for you, the prison warden is a megalomaniac with an obsession for mathematical riddles."

"Sounds all too plausible, old chap."

"You are offered a chance," Holmes continued loftily. "Your door contains a combination lock with five dials, each numbered 0 to 9. You may serve out your time peacefully, or you may tell the guard your guess for how many possible combinations there are for your lock. If your guess is correct within five per cent, you will be set free. If it is wrong, you will be put to death. What do you do?"

What I actually did was eat some more kipper, and ponder permutations. How many combinations do you think there are for the lock?

SOLUTION ON PAGE 102

The First Wordknot

As I was going through some medical textbooks one afternoon, hoping to confirm a diagnostic suspicion regarding a patient, Holmes accosted me bearing a slip of paper.

"Here," he told me urgently. "Take this."

I glanced at the paper. It bore the following message:

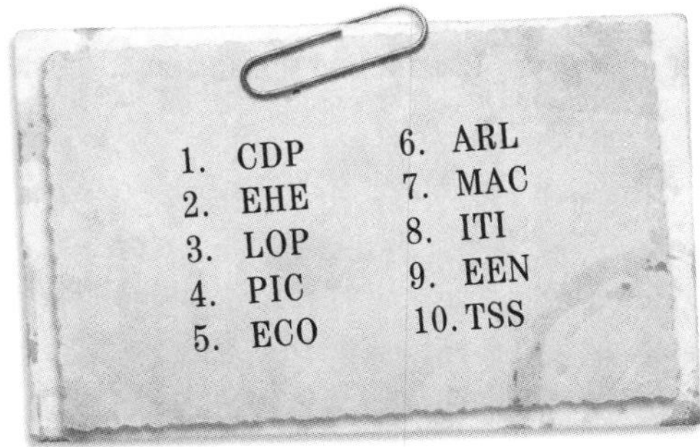
1. CDP
2. EHE
3. LOP
4. PIC
5. ECO
6. ARL
7. MAC
8. ITI
9. EEN
10. TSS

"What is it, Holmes? Some sort of devilish cipher?"

"Not too devilish, I trust," he told me. "There are three ten-letter words on this note. The first line bears their initial letters, the second their second letters, and so on, until the tenth line, which bears their final letters. However, on each line, the three letters are jumbled around. The words are linked by a loose theme. Can you find them?"

The penny dropped. "This is a test?"

"Obviously."

Can you find the three words?

SOLUTION ON PAGE 103

Whisky

I took a sip from my glass of whisky, and relaxed back into the armchair, enjoying the warmth of the merry fireplace in front of us. "This is excellent, Holmes."

He nodded. "As it should be, at seven shillings."

I winced. "Can you get anything back for the empty bottle?"

"Yes, the brandy is worth 80 pence more than the glass."

There are, of course, 12 pence to the shilling. How much was the bottle worth?

SOLUTION ON PAGE 103

Cousin Tracy

Having befuddled me with her candle purchases, Mrs Hudson proceeded to recount a lengthy and somewhat muddled story regarding her cousin Tracy, and Tracy's husband Albert. As best I could ascertain, both Tracy and Albert were on their second marriages, having lost their earlier spouses to illness, or possibly misadventure.

Clearly this shared loss proved a bond for the couple. The family now stretched to nine children in total, quite the brood. There was a certain amount of tension between his children, her children, and their children, and their shenanigans appeared to be the foundation of the anecdote.

From what I could glean from the mess of names and dates, Tracy and Albert each had six children whom they could call their own in a biological sense. Mrs Hudson neglected to specify how many had been born from the happy couple's union, and Holmes was quick to inform me that I ought to be able to work it out for myself.

Can you say how many were children of both Tracy and Albert?

SOLUTION ON PAGE 104

THE CANDLES

"There's something wrong with that new candle-boy," Mrs Hudson observed one morning, when she arrived to remove our breakfast things. "He absolutely refuses to deliver normal-sized boxes of candles."

Holmes sat up, evidently curious. "How so, Mrs Hudson?"

"He says he's only got six sizes of box, and he's not breaking them for nobody. It wouldn't be so bad if his boxes weren't so stupid."

"Oh?" I asked, now intrigued despite myself.

She nodded, clearly irritated just by the thought of it. "His boxes come in lots of 16, 17, 23, 24, 39, and 40 candles. That's all. They're all the same size. It's ridiculous. He says I have to make an order for specific amounts of the various boxes."

I smiled at her sympathetically. "And how many candles do you normally order, my dear lady?"

"One hundred," she said. "We go through them like nobody's business. I don't dare order them now, though."

Holmes snorted and sagged back into his chair, which I took to mean the end of his interest in the matter.

Could Mrs Hudson get her candles, and if so, what would she have to order?

25

SOLUTION ON PAGE 104

Passing By

T*he Adventure of the Wandering Bishops* saw Holmes and I on the train from Waterloo to Weychester one Tuesday morning. Our idle conversation was interrupted by a train rattling past loudly on the other track. Once it was clear, Holmes announced that the intruding train had been half our own train's length of 400 feet. I complimented him on his good eye for such things. I rather hoped that might close the matter, but as it transpired, I was wrong.

"I can tell you that it took the two trains just five seconds to pass each other in their entirety. Furthermore, if the two had been travelling in the same direction, the faster would have passed the slower in precisely 15 seconds."

"Is that so?" I hoped I managed to convey interest.

"Can you tell me what speed the faster of the two trains is running at? Feet per second will do perfectly well as a unit of measurement."

Can you find the solution?

SOLUTION ON PAGE 105

27

Trilogy

Mrs Hudson's final shot, after well over a quarter of an hour of the most baffling details of her cousin Tracy's extended family, was the strange fate of a loosely related in-law. Cousin Tracy's husband's brother's cousin-in-law's father, to be precise. This worthy, whose name I didn't catch, had apparently served in the Zulu War of '79. He had been exposed to some horrifying brutalities whilst out there, and on his return, was never quite the same.

Some years later, as Mrs Hudson would have it, the former soldier was at his parish church with wife and child, as was usual on a Sunday. On this ill-fated occasion, he dozen off quietly, falling into a terrible nightmare about being captured by the Zulus with the rest of his brigade. The Zulus began decapitating their prisoners one by one. In the dream, he was about to meet the same fate when his wife, realizing her husband was asleep, tapped him on the back of the neck with her fan to wake him up. The sudden shock overwhelmed his already stressed system, and he immediately dropped stone dead.

This was the point at which Holmes rose from his seat and politely but forcefully thanked Mrs Hudson for breakfast, and ushered her out of our rooms. Closing the door behind her, Holmes muttered, "Blatant piffle!" He then stalked off in high dudgeon, and moments later the sounds of aggrieved violin-playing filled the air.

Why did Holmes disbelieve Mrs Hudson?

SOLUTION ON PAGE

Buckets

I was cleaning my pipe one evening, with my revolver shortly to follow, when Holmes appeared in my peripheral vision and placed a big metal bucket in front of me with a loud clang. I startled, turning to look at him as I pulled backwards.

"Water," Holmes declared.

"I'm fine for the moment, thanks," I told him as patiently as I was able.

"You misunderstand," he said.

I nodded glumly. "I dare say I do."

"Two identical buckets, filled to the precise brim with water." He paused. "Pray engage your imagination. This empty one is by way of illustration."

"Done," I said. "Although I dare say I could have managed the feat without a real-world model."

"Reassuring to hear," Holmes said. "Now, one of the buckets has a large chunk of wood floating in it. The precise shape does not matter."

"Very well."

"Which of your two buckets weighs more, the one with the wood, or the one without?"

What do you think?

SOLUTION ON PAGE 106

The Maddened Miller

One of the odder features of *The Adventure of the Wandering Bishops* was a peculiarly enraged Hookland miller. The source of his ire was, we eventually discovered, an altercation between his wife and her sister, which disrupted certain plans he had regarding the purchase of a large quantity of land. But that really is by the by.

Holmes, still in his farmer's disguise, had approached the miller with several sacks of grain, purchased earlier in return for a dozen chickens. The miller's usual tariff was one tenth part of the flour he produced for any given customer. Holmes, of course, was only too happy to pay this trifling price.

When the work was done, we found ourselves in possession of a bushel of freshly ground flour. The less said about that, the better. But my question is this. How much flour did the enraged miller claim?

SOLUTION ON PAGE 

THE PAINTING

A fellow came to me once looking to sell a rather handsome portrait that had been in his family for some time. This was nothing to do with a case of Holmes'. He was a patient of mine at my practice, and had noticed that I had a selection of artworks adorning the walls of my office and treatment room.

Whilst the picture was undeniably attractive, his asking price was not – £640. Well, half a year's income is a ludicrous amount of money for a piece of art, so of course I declined pleasantly. Two weeks later he was back, and had dropped his asking price to a "mere" £400. Once again, I conveyed my regrets. After two more weeks, he returned, utterly unabashed, and offered me the piece for £250. On his second visit after that, I finally gave in and purchased the piece.

To the nearest whole pound, how much did I pay?

SOLUTION ON PAGE 107

31

The First Camouflage

I remember the day clearly, even now. It was late October, a Friday. We had finished luncheon a short while before, and I was sitting in a pleasant state of post-prandial sleepiness. I was on the verge of nodding off when Holmes loudly called out, "I've got four words for you, Watson."

I think I managed some groan of mild protest, which Holmes duly ignored.

"Elephantine. Beechwood. Bugleweed. Stepmother."

"And?" I asked.

"Each word contains a smaller word, well camouflaged within its parent. What is the common theme uniting the four smaller words?"

It was definitely not the way that I'd fondly imagined my afternoon progressing. Can you find the solution?

SOLUTION ON PAGE

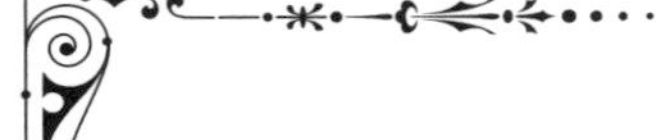

FABULOUS

"Hubris, Watson, is one of the very heights of folly. To become so swollen with arrogance that one assumes oneself infallible – and to act or, more pertinently, fail to act as a result of that arrogance – why, that is the cause of inevitable disaster."

"Is that so?" I asked, somewhat confused.

Holmes waved a newspaper at me. "Some buffoon of a runner was so overconfident about his opponent that he opened himself to utter ridicule. According to this piece, our fellow gave his inferior rival a head-start equal to one-eighth of the length of the course. Now, they started at opposite ends for some reason, and after his late start, the superior runner ambled along with colossal contempt for his opponent. He got a nasty shock when, at just one-sixth of the way along the course, he met his rival coming the other way. He lost, of course." Holmes paused, and a glint appeared in his eye.

"Quite so," I said swiftly.

"Maybe you can tell me, old chap, how many times the buffoon would have had to increase his speed in order to win the race? Round to the nearest whole number, and let's assume that the slower man maintains the same speed throughout."

What do you think?

33

SOLUTION ON PAGE

OUT EAST

Whilst doing some research during *The Nasty Affair of the Highwayman's Daughter*, I stumbled across an interesting little snippet of fact about her father's home country. It was a small, mountainous state in eastern Europe of no great political or cultural distinction, with a reputation for sullen bloodthirstiness amongst its menfolk. No great surprise, given the context in which I was examining it.

Be that as it may, the discovery I made was that in the preceding year, some 1.4 per cent of the country's women as compared to 2.1 per cent of the men had married spouses of the same nationality.

I announced this to Holmes, who immediately challenged me to deduce the comparative percentage of women in that place.

What do you think?

SOLUTION ON PAGE

35

The Suicide

Inspector Lestrade of Scotland Yard was a small, lean man with a strong hint of ferret in his ancestry. Whilst his approach to crime was wholly pedestrian, he was nevertheless a tireless servant of the law. Holmes and I worked with him a number of times to bring villains to justice. Despite having received ample evidence of Holmes' brilliance however, he somehow maintained an intrinsic faith in his own opinion when it differed. So I was utterly unsurprised, during *The Adventure of the Impossible Gecko*, when he dismissed Holmes' first analysis out of hand.

"Look, Holmes, I understand that your client fears foul play. But it's a suicide, clear and simple. There's nothing here to suggest otherwise." Lestrade gestured around the study we were in. "The only thing we've moved is the deceased."

It was a dim little room, lined with book-filled cases and dominated by a leather-topped oak desk and the chair that went with it. In the centre of the desk sat a pill bottle, completely empty. The remaining couple of pills lay next to it, big white oblong things about the same size as the tip of my little finger. The rest of the bottle – 20 pills or more – had gone into our client's uncle the night before. The only other thing in the room was a sheet of financial projections, which appeared utterly dire.

"My point precisely," Holmes said, with a hint of asperity. "Surely even you, Inspector, can see that suicide is highly unlikely at the very least."

He was right, of course. Can you see what he'd spotted?

SOLUTION ON PAGE 110

SCARVES

One blustery autumn afternoon, Holmes and I were walking along the Marylebone Road, past Madame Tussauds' museum of wax figures. I was struggling somewhat to keep my hat in place when a particularly savage gust whipped it straight off my head. As I stooped to retrieve it, I noticed that a lady in front of us had likewise lost her scarf, which went tumbling away down the pavement.

Holmes had noticed the errant scarf as well, and turned to me with a calculating look. "Indulge me a moment, Watson, and picture that the street was significantly more crowded, and that there were a dozen ladies who found themselves suddenly without their scarves. For that matter, let's also imagine that young Wiggins was nearby, had gathered up all the scarves, and was handing them back at random to the ladies, in hope of a penny or two for his speedy service."

Wiggins was the spokesman and putative leader of the Baker Street Irregulars, a gaggle of urchins that Holmes often recruited when in need of extra eyes or hands.

"It doesn't seem impossible," I allowed, although knowing the lad, I very much doubted he'd be quite so careless as to return the scarves randomly.

"Well, then," Holmes said, "can you calculate the probability of just 11 of the ladies receiving their correct scarves?"

To my mild surprise, I realized that I could. Can you?

SOLUTION ON PAGE 110

JOE

"I asked my nephew Joseph how old he was last Saturday," Mrs Hudson declared, having brought up some hot tea one afternoon. "You'll never believe what he told me, Doctor Watson."

"I'm sure I shall," I reassured her. "I trust you implicitly, my dear lady."

She gave me a queer look, before continuing. "He told me, bold as brass, that three years ago he'd been seven times as old as his sister Ruthie. Then he added that two years ago, he'd been four times her age, and one year ago, just three times her age. After that outburst, he sat back and beamed at me. Well, I'm sure you'll have no trouble figuring out their ages, a learned man like yourself, but it wasn't what I was expecting, not at all." She beamed at me in turn.

Fortunately, long association with Sherlock Holmes had hardened me to this sort of challenge, and I was able to respond. Can you calculate the answer?

SOLUTION ON PAGE 111

THE WENNS

Holmes and I were lurking outside a small hotel named The Wenns in the quiet fenland town of King's Lynn. It was perhaps one of the less diverting ways of spending a Monday evening, but we were hot on the heels of the frightened carpenter's brother-in-law, whom Holmes needed to observe in the wild, as it were. The little marketplace was quaint enough, to be sure, but as the evening dragged on, I confess I was becoming rather bored.

Catching my mood, Holmes decided to give my mind something to chew on, by way of a distraction from the drizzle. "You'll have observed that the bar in there is quite crowded, Watson."

"Quite so," I replied. "Warm and dry too, no doubt."

"Indubitably. Still, let us pretend that each of the patrons has a different number of penny coins in his possession, and that there are more patrons by number than any single one of them has pennies."

There was a pause whilst I untangled this, and then I nodded.

"Now, if I tell you that none of the patrons possesses exactly 33 pennies, can you tell me how many patrons there are at most?"

"I'm sure I can, in theory at least," I replied.

"Then please do so," he said.

What is the correct answer?

SOLUTION ON PAGE 111

Maida Vale

During *The Adventure of the Maida Vale Baker*, Holmes tasked Wiggins and the Irregulars with observing both the baker, Gerry by name, and his dissolute cousin, James. Caution was strictly advised, as both men were prone to a certain lamentable rashness.

When Wiggins returned to 221b, he reported that Gerry had left the bakery at 9 a.m. sharp, and set off up Watling Street at a leisurely two miles an hour. An hour later, James had followed in his cousin's footsteps, but walking more briskly, at four miles an hour, and with a lovely Irish setter in tow.

The dog had immediately dashed off after the baker, and according to Wiggins's intelligence, had no sooner caught up to Gerry than it turned around and ran back to James. It then proceeded to continue running back and forth between the men – at an even ten miles per hour – until James had caught up with Gerry, at which point all three stopped entirely.

We made sense of it all in the end, but how far did the dog run?

SOLUTION ON PAGE

SHEEP

The thorny particulars of the inheritability of sheep became a pressing concern for Holmes and myself during the frankly rather peculiar *Adventure of the Raven Child*, which unfolded largely in the mountains of Gwynedd. A landowner with a heroic combined flock of sheep had died in bizarre circumstances after spending a night alone at the top of Cader Idris – a feat said by the locals to turn you into either a poet or a madman. As if there were a difference.

Anyhow, for the purposes of this volume, I shall spare you the convoluted details, and instead focus on the practical issue of sheep herds. The landowner's sons, David, Idris, and Caradog, all inherited a portion of their father's herd, along with the lands and tenant shepherds required to support the sheep. David, as the eldest, received 20 per cent more sheep than Idris, and 25 per cent more sheep than Caradog, the youngest brother.

If I tell you that Idris received precisely 1,000 sheep, can you tell me how many Caradog inherited?

SOLUTION ON PAGE 112

The Second Wordknot

If I recall correctly – and I am reasonably sure that I do – I was engaged in the precarious business of attempting to butter a very hot crumpet when Holmes presented me with my second wordknot. It was some weeks since I'd wrestled with the first of its kind, but the simple principle of untangling three loosely associated ten-letter words was still reasonably fresh.

"You recall, I assume, that the first letter of each word is on the first line, the second letter of each on the second line, and so on?"

I assured Holmes that I so recalled, and with that he left me to it.

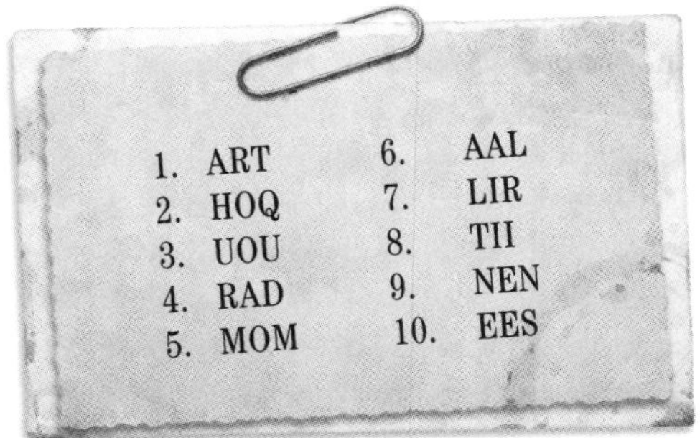
1. ART
2. HOQ
3. UOU
4. RAD
5. MOM
6. AAL
7. LIR
8. TII
9. NEN
10. EES

Can you untangle the knot?

SOLUTION ON PAGE 113

THE PARTNER

Much of the nastiness surrounding *The Adventure of the Maida Vale Baker* was rooted in his business affairs. It is often the case, I have found, that the trust one places in family and friends is misplaced when it comes to affairs of the wallet. The baker, Gerry, and his cousin James had been partners in the bakery since the beginning. James provided the capital, whilst Gerry did the work and ran the business. Once the basic investment capital had been repaid, they settled on an agreement whereby Gerry owned one and a half times as much of the business as James did.

Matters did not start to get complicated until a new arrival appeared on the scene. Mr Andreas was a contact of James, a friend of a friend. A gentleman of Greek extraction, he was possessed of a certain presence that warned the discerning onlooker not to trifle with him. Sadly, neither James nor Gerry apparently had sufficient discernment.

The deal they struck was that Mr Andreas would pay the handsome sum of £1,000, and each of the three partners would then hold a one-third stake in the business. Matters quickly became unseemly.

What would have been the most equitable distribution of the money, £1,000?

SOLUTION ON PAGE 113

FRUITY

On occasion, Mrs Hudson enjoyed presenting Holmes with some small test of ingenuity, if for no other satisfaction than to take a perverse pride in how rapidly he was able to respond. Sometimes, Holmes would pass the onus of response to me, either because he deemed the matter beneath his weighty appraisal, or because of his ongoing attempts to improve my logical processes. Mrs Hudson seemed scarcely less pleased on those occasions. I assume that whatever she lost by way of Holmes' rapier mind, she made up for by watching me fumble around trying to best her.

One morning, before I'd even been able to take a cup of tea, one such conundrum winged its way towards me. I pulled myself together, looked up from my cup, and said, "I'm sorry, Mrs Hudson, could you repeat that?"

"Of course, Doctor," she replied. "I was weighing the fruit earlier, for a crumble, and it hit me. One apple and six plums were the same weight as my one pear, while all three apples and the pear were the same weight as ten plums. So I was wondering, how many plums do you think would match the weight of the pear?"

"Thank you," I said, and took a long, slow drink of tea.

What do you think the answer is?

SOLUTION ON PAGE 114

CIDER

Whilst in Hookland on *The Adventure of the Wandering Bishops*, Holmes made the mistake of impressing a voluble cider manufacturer with his insight. The fellow then commenced to ply us both with questions ranging from blatantly simple to utterly baffling. Most seemed to have at least some practical application. Holmes was in disguise at the time, and was forced to grit his teeth and indulge the persistent – and tipsy – fellow to avoid causing a scene. Finally he moved on, but not before both of us had comprehensively run out of patience.

One of his questions has stayed with me, perhaps because it was at least comprehensible. In the course of planting a new, square orchard with evenly spaced young trees, the fellow discovered that he had 146 trees left over unplanted. He needed to obtain a further 31 trees in order to plant them all and still have a square orchard.

How many trees had he already planted?

SOLUTION ON PAGE 114

HANDS

We were introduced to an inordinately large number of people during *The Adventure of the Frightened Carpenter*. At one point, it was starting to feel as if I was going to have to personally shake hands with everybody in London. Given that several of them had insisted on attempting to crush my hand to pulp as part of the process, I was rapidly tiring of the whole affair, and made some throwaway remark to Holmes to that effect.

"Don't disparage the humble handshake, Watson," Holmes told me. "It's a vital part of the social glue that holds the city together, no matter how tiresome it might prove on occasion. Consider yourself grateful that we are not in a culture where a crushing grip is the standard of politesse."

"Oh, I am," I assured him.

"Here's a little something to take your mind off your manual weariness. Do you imagine that there are an odd or even number of people who have themselves shaken hands with an odd number of people?"

Can you deduce an answer?

SOLUTION ON PAGE 115

A Sense of Urgency

Holmes inevitably seized a moment when I was at my most distracted before springing his little tests and puzzles upon me. I asked him about this once, and his reply was something to the effect that observation and deduction were frequently required at times when the pressure was greatest. By interrupting me when my mind was elsewhere, he hoped to strengthen my logical faculties to work under duress. I could see the sense in it, but it was often damnably inconvenient.

I was in the middle of making notes upon an intriguing yet highly convoluted article in *The Lancet* when Holmes dashed over with a scrap of paper and thrust it under my nose. He even made his voice sound concerned. "Quick, Watson! Hurry! What's the answer?"

The paper bore this inscription:

10*9*8*7*6*5*4*3*2*1*0*–1*–2 = X

What's X?

SOLUTION ON PAGE 115

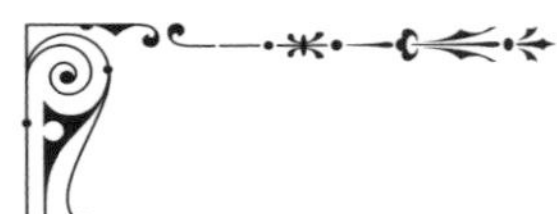

Hot and Cold

Sherlock and I were taking tea one chilly January morning when he looked up from studying his cup, to turn his attention to the frosty window. "We place a kettle or a pot on top of the hob in order to heat up. In earlier times, people hung their cauldrons and kettles over fireplaces. Not right in the middle of them, but over them."

"Quite so," I agreed. "More convenient or more effective. Or both."

"Both," he agreed. "But imagine for a moment that you have a cube of metal, say, that you wish to cool, and a block of ice that you have to keep intact. How would you arrange the two for greatest efficiency?"

"Well, I'd..." I trailed off, to think about the matter.

What is the best option?

SOLUTION ON PAGE 116

On the Buses

During *The Affair of the Frightened Carpenter*, Holmes had cause to invest some time in studying the movements of a fellow named Sam Smith. It left Holmes somewhat waspish, because it transpired that Smith was in the frugal habit of travelling by bus to his appointments, and walking back from them on foot.

On the second day, the combined travel time was precisely eight hours. Holmes also had to spend 90 minutes loitering outside a lumber merchant's depot, but that's by the by. Given that the bus managed an average of 9 mph, and Smith's walking rate was a third of that, how far did Holmes have to walk while trailing the man?

SOLUTION ON PAGE 116

HOOKLAND KNIGHTS

A lead followed during *The Adventure of the Wandering Bishops* brought us to a rather unusual under-chapel below the streets of Weychester. Three sarcophagi carved to look like armoured crusader knights dominated a small room off the main chapel.

Beneath the feet of each knight was a set of finely carved numbers. On the first was the group 30, 68, 89. On the second, the numbers 18, 23, 42. The third bore the numbers 11, 41, 74.

At the end of the small room, the wall held a dozen carved stone heads in a straight line across its middle. Each of the heads was clearly modelled after a different individual. Every face bore an expression of unsettling glee, however. It was most unpleasant. Above the heads was painted the number 16, in white, a good foot high.

"Clearly, a reference to..." Holmes stopped mid-sentence. "Watson, this should exercise you. Which knight is that painted number pointing us to?"

SOLUTION ON PAGE 117

The Third Wordknot

Holmes' third wordknot came to me as we sat down to suffer through a thoroughly uninspired performance of an already lacklustre operetta. Normally you would never have found either of us within 50 feet of such a performance, but Holmes was on the trail of a decrepit raven-seller, and, well, there we were. I was actually glad of the distraction his puzzle afforded me, even though the unfortunate wailings made it difficult to concentrate.

The letters from which I had to disentangle three related ten-letter words, one letter each per line, were:

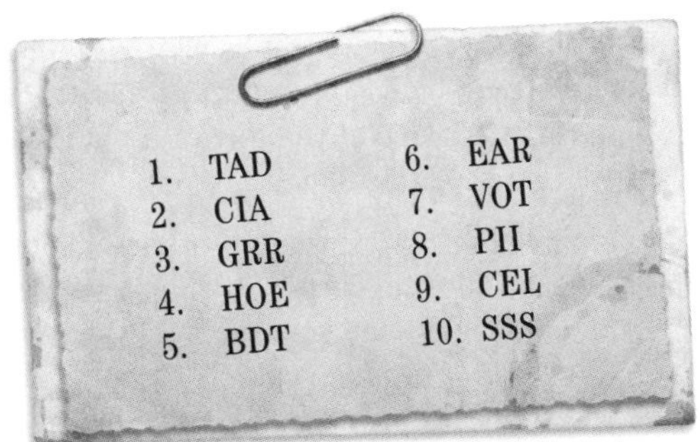

1. TAD
2. CIA
3. GRR
4. HOE
5. BDT
6. EAR
7. VOT
8. PII
9. CEL
10. SSS

Can you work out what the words were?

SOLUTION ON PAGE 118

DANIEL

I was reading the newspaper one afternoon when a rather grizzly little news story caught my eye. It concerned the unfortunate fate of one Daniel Boutros, the son of a rather wealthy shipping broker.

Young Mr Boutros had been to Essex on a climbing trip with a companion. Despite being generally considered skilled at the sport, something had gone wrong, and he had fallen from the top of an escarpment. His friend Alan Dickey, the lead climber, had already reached the top and was belaying Boutros from up there when the rope failed.

This was, of course, very sad, but what startled me were the florid lengths to which the newspaper reporter went in describing the scene. Several paragraphs were devoted in their entirety to poor Boutros's body, and the way it lay shattered over the mounds of coiled rope at the foot of the cliff. The friend, Dickey, was said to be in shock.

I mentioned the piece to Holmes, who grunted noncommittally. After a moment, he asked if there was any mention of a frayed rope-end. I scanned through, and sure enough, the reporter did mention frayed pieces of unwound rope.

"It's still murder," Holmes said.

Can you see why he came to that conclusion?

SOLUTION ON PAGE 118

STRAIGHTFORWARD PUZZLES

"Crime is common.
Logic is rare."

Sherlock Holmes

The Pleasant Lake

The Peculiar Case of the Raven Child **dragged Holmes and myself up to the Gwynedd village of Abergynolwyn. A devilishly long way to go, but Holmes insisted we had to see some details for ourselves. So one grey morning, we found ourselves in a small chapel on the shores of a glacial lake, the Tal-y-Llyn, where the River Dysynni begins.**

Inside the chapel, a simple altar bore an exhortation regarding the Ten Commandments, along with the customary cloth and Bible. Above it, on the wall, a curious message was chiselled, clearly of some age:

P R S V R Y P R F C T M N
V R K P T H S P R C P T S T

Holmes glanced at it, and his eyes narrowed for a moment. Then he turned to me, with a certain light in his eye. "That last line is missing a final 'N'," he said.

"Clearly that's not all that's missing," I replied.

"I'll grant you that," he said. "There's precisely one other letter missing too – more than a dozen copies of it."

He would say no more, and we had to sit there until I'd decoded the message. It was not a comfortable time. Can you tell what the message is?

SOLUTION ON PAGE 122

The Uncle

We were walking through the cemetery at Paddington Green, looking for the headstone of a carpenter's uncle. There was some doubt as to the date of that worthy's final repose, and we had resolved to go straight to the source. As it transpired, our efforts were fruitless. Secretly, the man had been alive for years, living with another family in Hadleigh.

As we passed a rather extravagant carving of an old, bearded man in a humble robe, Holmes nodded to himself.

"Here's a simple little matter for you to chew on, Watson."

I nodded. "Very well, old chap."

"Let us posit that a particular fellow has spent a fifth of his life as a child, a quarter as a youth, a third as a man, and 13 years in decline. How old must he be?"

Can you find the answer?

SOLUTION ON PAGE

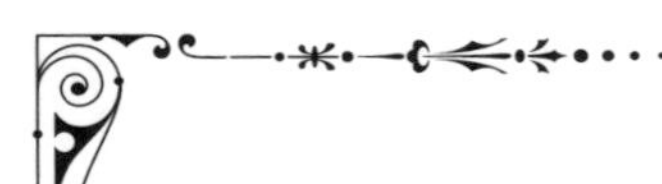

Slick

Picking my way cautiously down Baker Street in the icy February morning was always a trying experience. It didn't help much that Holmes often appeared to have the feet of a cat, and hardly ever slipped around. I, on the other hand, typically felt in serious danger of crashing to the ground with every step I took.

One morning, Holmes took note of my stumbling and suggested that I attempt to walk on the slickest, smoothest patches of ice I could find, rather than preferring those patches with a little texture to offer grip.

I, in turn, suggested that I was having enough trouble as it was.

"But, my dear chap, you'll find the smooth stuff easier to walk on than the rough. The smoother, the better."

He was right, as he inevitably is. Can you say why?

SOLUTION ON PAGE 123

The Second Camouflage

I was sorting through my pocket change, which had become annoyingly weighty, when Holmes inflicted his second set of camouflage words on me. "Heartbreaker, journeyers, solipsistic and diagnoses," he declared. Having pulled my wits together and confirmed that I was supposed to locate the four small, thematically linked words hiding within each of the longer ones, I had him repeat them to me.

Can you find the answer?

SOLUTION ON PAGE 123

Forty-Five

Holmes picked a slice of toast from the breakfast rack, but instead of buttering it, he thoughtfully tore it into four uneven pieces, and tossed them onto the tray.

"Mrs Hudson won't like that, old chap," I warned him. "You know how she is about food vandalism."

"Forty-five," he replied.

I blinked.

"Curious number," he said. "Of course, they all are."

"Of course," I muttered, under my breath.

"You can split 45 into four chunks, four different natural numbers that added together produce it as their total. So far, so true of anything over nine. But these particular four numbers are somewhat special. Add two to the first, subtract two from the second, the third multiply by two, and the fourth divide by two. The result of each four operations is the same. Can you tell me the numbers?"

"I dare say," I replied. "May I finish my egg first?"

"If you must."

What are the four numbers in question?

SOLUTION ON PAGE 123

61

ST MARY AXE

Holmes was reading a file that Inspector Lestrade had furnished him with some high-profile matter regarding purloined diaries belonging to a cabinet minister's younger daughter. Every so often, he'd snort or toss his head, rather like an ill-tempered stallion. Finally, he put the papers down, and turned to me. "Lestrade's documents say that Mr Lloyd takes precisely four hours to walk to and from his home in Stoke Newington to the City, not counting the 60 seconds he takes to hand an envelope to a small man in St Mary Axe. His outward journey is conducted at an average rate of five miles per hour, and the return journey three."

"Is that useful to know?" I asked innocently.

"Not in the least," Holmes replied. "Maybe you'd tell me how far it is from Lloyd's home to his small man in the city?"

Can you find the answer?

SOLUTION ON PAGE 124

GREAT-AUNT ADA

Mrs Hudson's steely gaze flicked to the mangled toast on the tray, and her eyes narrowed. "Have I ever told you gentlemen about my Great-Aunt Ada?" she asked, her voice deceptively mild.

I winced, and shook my head. "I don't believe so, Mrs Hudson."

"She's 45 years older than I am. Always has been, of course. But she's getting a little long in the tooth, and this year, if you take her age and swap the digits, you end up with my age. Curious." She paused for a moment. "Both the digits are primes, too," she added primly.

Holmes just snorted, leaving me to work out her Great-Aunt Ada's age. Can you do it?

SOLUTION ON PAGE 125

Ronnie

Mrs Hudson was in high dudgeon over the supposedly high-handed way that one of her cousins, a gardener out in the Home Counties, had been treated by his latest employer.

"Ronnie agreed an annual salary of £500 plus a rather nice all-weather cape with the Terringtons. In the end, he had to leave them after seven months, because my Uncle Hob had a nasty turn. The Terringtons gave him just £60, on top of the cape. Sixty quid! That's less than ten pounds a month. It's a disgrace."

"That's dreadful," I sympathized, but I'll admit that at the same time, I was wondering precisely how expensive the cape actually was.

Assuming the Terringtons are playing fair, what's the cape worth?

SOLUTION ON PAGE 125

FEBRUARY

I was reading *The Times* of London when Holmes, having glanced at the date on the front of the paper, said, "Did you know that the last time we had a February with five Wednesdays in it was in 1888?"

Having given myself a moment to process this information, I confirmed that no, in fact I had not been consciously aware of that fact.

"It may interest you to calculate when the next occasion will be," Holmes continued.

Whilst I did not feel that the matter was especially fascinating, I went ahead and worked it out. Can you?

SOLUTION ON PAGE 126

The Code

We came across an encrypted sales ledger whilst investigating *The Adventure of the Frightened Carpenter*. It wasn't especially challenging to decode, but it was interesting, so I shall present a sample to you here for your amusement and possible edification:

GAUNT+
OILER=
\------
RGUOEI

The trick to the code was reasonably straightforward. The fellow had selected a common ten-letter English word, one in which all the letters were different, and then assigned the digits from 1 up to 9 and then 0 to the letters. He then simply substituted the appropriate letter for each digit.

On that basis, can you find the key word?

SOLUTION ON PAGE 126

ISAAC

"Catch!" Holmes tossed an apple in my general direction.

I caught it shortly before it struck me in the chest.

He nodded. "You know, I trust, that everything falls at the same speed?"

"Well, I seem to remember hearing something of the sort," I replied. "But drop a tumbler of Scotch and a piece of paper, and tell me that again."

Holmes smiled. "Experimentation. Good. I should say then, that apart from the effects of air resistance, everything falls at the same speed. Gravity pulls on every atom of an object simultaneously, not just the ones on the outer surface."

"Hmm," I said. "Well, if you say so. It seems a little counter-intuitive, however."

"Indeed it does, Watson. Indeed it does. So, experimentation. Can you devise an experiment we can perform here and now?"

SOLUTION ON PAGE 127

THE TRACK

Our pursuit of the dubious Alan Grey, whom we encountered during *The Adventure of the Third Carriage*, led Holmes and myself to a circular running track where, as the sun fell, we witnessed a race using bicycles. There was some sort of substantial wager involved in the matter, as I recall, and the track had been closed off specially for the occasion. This was insufficient to prevent our ingress, obviously.

One of the competitors was wearing red, and the other blue. We never did discover their names. As the race started, red immediately pulled ahead. A few moments later, Holmes observed that if they maintained their pace, red would complete a lap in four minutes, whilst blue would complete one in seven.

Having made that pronouncement, he turned to me. "How long would it be before red passed blue if they kept those rates up, old chap?"

Whilst I wrestled with the answer, Holmes went back to watching the proceedings.

Can you find the solution?

SOLUTION ON PAGE 128

A Chelsea Tale

"My Angie's fella, Trevor," said Mrs Hudson, "He's got a pal named Rick, and it was Rick's sister Sally who told me about the brother of her cousin's best friend, Roderick."

"Um, is that the cousin, the best friend, or the brother?" I asked, starting to sink.

Mrs Hudson gave me a very pitying look. "Roddie? He's Budgie's friend. Lovely lad, he is, specially considering."

I thought about asking what I was supposed to consider, but decided discretion in this instance was the better part of valour.

"Anyhow," she continued. "Roddie knows this guy who works out in Chelsea, if you can believe it."

That seemed entirely plausible, and I nodded accordingly.

"Well, Sally was telling me that Jez – that's the Chelsea chap, Doctor – got such a nasty fright at work the other day from a gigantic hornet the size of a robin that he leapt straight through the window he was standing at. It's eight floors up, Doctor."

"That's terrible," I said, genuinely shocked. "Poor man."

"Yes. He was sacked straight away, of course."

"Wait," I said, swinging back to total confusion. "What? Sacked? Wasn't he killed?"

"Killed? Not hardly. He has a small cut on his ear from the glass, but no, otherwise he was totally fine."

"I don't understand," I had to confess.

Do you?

SOLUTION ON PAGE 

70

EXPRESS

Holmes and I were on the Waterloo train, out of Westchester. It was a slow service for a non-stopping express, managing a speed of precisely 40 miles per hour, or so Holmes assured me anyway. We'd been travelling for a little over an hour when a train in the opposite direction thundered past, heading into Hookland. That one, he informed me, was the faster express, travelling at 60 miles an hour, having left Waterloo more than two hours before.

By this point, I was anticipating a test of my reasoning, possibly algebraic in nature, and Holmes didn't disappoint.

"How far apart were the two trains an hour ago, Watson?"

Can you find the answer?

SOLUTION ON PAGE 129

The Fence

Wiggins, the chief scamp of the Baker Street Irregulars, was reporting to us regarding movements afoot in Highgate Cemetery. He looked unusually weary, but no less alert or mischievous for that.

"They're putting up some sort of statue, Mr Holmes," the boy said.

"I knew it," Holmes replied. "Are they fencing it off?"

"They are, sir. But they're having trouble."

Holmes perked up. "Oh? How so?"

"Well, they clearly want to use all the posts they have, and make an even fence. I heard one of 'em moaning that at a foot apart, they had 150 posts too few, whilst at a yard, they had 70 too many."

Our discussion went on for some time, but let me ask you this – how many posts did the would-be fencers have?

SOLUTION ON PAGE 129

The Fourth Wordknot

Holmes and I were in a comfortable tea-house with a clear line of sight to the front doors of St Paul's Cathedral. ***The Adventure of the Impossible Gecko*** **had taken an unexpectedly clerical turn, and some extended observation was in order. When Holmes handed me a slip of paper, I at first mistakenly assumed it was something to do with the matter at hand. Not so. It was the fourth wordknot.**

"You know the drill, Watson. Three loosely linked ten-letter words, first letters jumbled on the first row, you have to unpick them."

"Quite," I said, taking the paper. It read:

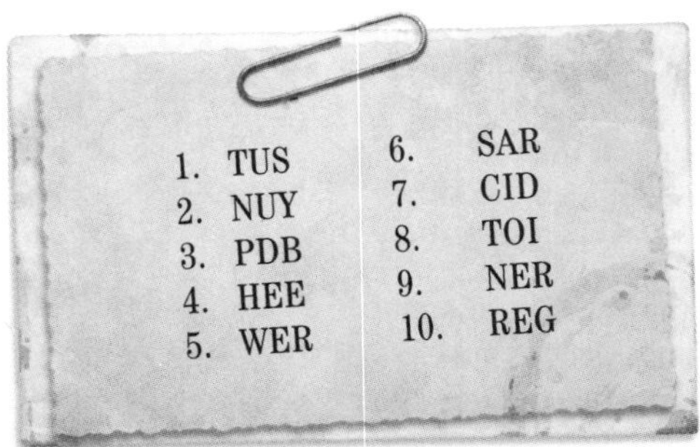

1. TUS
2. NUY
3. PDB
4. HEE
5. WER
6. SAR
7. CID
8. TOI
9. NER
10. REG

Can you find the solution?

SOLUTION ON PAGE 130

The One

"Many numbers have plausible claims to interest," Holmes told me.

I nodded, passingly familiar with some of the eccentricities of the mathematician's art.

"This one, however, is quite unique. Can you perhaps tell me why?"

He handed me a notepad, on which he had written the number 8,549,176,320.

Do you know what he was getting at?

SOLUTION ON PAGE 130

BISCUITS

Wiggins told us about an altercation amongst the Irregulars which had fallen to him to mediate. A small sack of biscuits had gone missing from their collective supplies, and it could have been any one of six suspects.

When he discussed the matter with the six, their stories boiled down to the following six statements:

Will: Stephen did it.

Max: Robin did it.

Mary: Will did it.

Stephen: I didn't do it.

Gwen: Max did it.

Robin: Yeah, Max did it.

His main annoyance with the affair was that only one of the six had told him the truth. He immediately discerned the guilty party from that, of course. Can you?

SOLUTION ON PAGE 131

Dangerous Ladies

Holmes watched Mrs Hudson depart from our rooms with a somewhat rueful expression. "On the subject of redoubtable women, Watson, I have a little mental exercise for you. Two of the most formidable women in ancient history were undoubtedly Cleopatra, the last pharaoh of Egypt, and our very own Boadicea, who razed Colchester, London and St Albans to the ground."

"My word," I said. "There's a lesson there, Holmes – don't mess with a Norfolk lass."

He shot me a dark look before continuing. "Our best estimates say that the two ladies had a combined lifespan of 69 years. We know that Cleopatra died in 30 BC, and that Boadicea's death came 129 years after Cleopatra's birth. So when was Boadicea born?"

Can you find the answer?

SOLUTION ON PAGE 131

SQUARE SHEEP

"Intuition," Holmes told me, "is just a way of saying that your brain spotted an answer that your conscious mind did not. It can be a powerful aid to deduction for those in whom the awareness is less than perfectly honed, provided that you are ever-vigilant for the differences between a genuine intuition and simple imagination. Telling the two apart is a matter of practice."

So saying, he tossed me a box of matches. "Thanks," I said, somewhat doubtfully.

"Four of those, Watson, will make you a square. If you fancy a practical application, imagine that they are fences, and you are marking off a pen for a sheep or goat. Better yet, let us say that each match is the equivalent of a yard in length, in which case our square is one square yard in area."

"Square sheep, perhaps?" I offered.

"Say rather enormously fat sheep. Your challenge is to discover the minimum number of matches required to make a closed shape of at least ten square yards in area – a pen for ten of your obese sheep. You are not allowed to break the matches, by the by."

It took me a lot of trial and error before Holmes was satisfied with my efforts.

Can you find a solution?

SOLUTION ON PAGE 132

MR ANDREAS

During *The Adventure of the Maida Vale Baker*, we had to look into the financial affairs of Mr Andreas. They proved quite surprisingly regular, in the mathematical sense of the word. Some 15 years before, the man had started an investment firm with his capital, of £1,600. His wealth then proceeded to grow by exactly 55 per cent every three years. It was quite uncanny how precise this was.

There was a reason for that, of course.

But for now, can you say to the nearest pound how much money Mr Andreas had after 15 years?

SOLUTION ON PAGE 133

The Bottle

Holmes said something quiet, and I looked up to see a bottle arcing through the air towards me. Luckily I had my hands free, so I managed to catch it, rather than just being clunked in the chest. It was clear glass, with a flat, circular base and straight sides which led up to a complicated, twisty neck, and a stoppered opening. It was about one-third full of water, or something that looked like water anyway.

"Well caught, Watson," said Holmes in a more normal volume. I frowned at him.

"I see that there is a ruler beside you," he continued. "Without opening the bottle or immersing it in any way, can you tell me the volume of liquid that it would hold when full?"

I was able to do so. Would you have been so able?

SOLUTION ON PAGE 133

HOW MANY COWS?

During *The Adventure of the Wandering Bishops,* Holmes disguised himself as a Hookland farmer, and demonstrated an astonishing mastery of the frankly baffling local dialect. On those occasions where he had conversations with his supposed peers – as happened with alarming regularity – I was frequently left at a complete loss as to the topic of discussion. Still, our subterfuge proved a very useful necessity in coming to grips with the elusive self-professed major, C. L. Nolan, and his trail of intrigue and terror. But I must not permit myself to get distracted.

After one encounter with a fellow with the unlikely name of Podge, Holmes confessed that they'd been discussing theoretical cows.

"Mr Podge seemed most concerned regarding his black woodland cow," he told me. "He said that this beast had started producing one female calf a year, from the age of two, and to his apparent distress, each of these female calves had grown to follow the exact pattern of their mother, as had their own offspring, and so on. He was particularly worried about the time, 25 years from the birth of the black woodland cow, when apparently 'the time would be right', whatever that may denote."

"My word," I said. "Queer fellow. Wouldn't half of them have died of old age, or been eaten, or something?"

"He seemed to think that they would all – of some inevitability – still be alive. How many female cows would we be talking about at this point?"

Can you find the answer?

SOLUTION ON PAGE 134

THE WATCH

***The Adventure of the Frightened Carpenter* led Holmes and myself to a warehouse. One of the more interesting things about that operation was the somewhat convoluted schedule that the four watchmen had devised for themselves. Their employers required that each man work two six-hour shifts a day with a break in between, starting precisely on the hour, so that there were always two men on duty, and both never changed shift at the same time.**

As we discovered later, each of the four men had their own personal requirements regarding their working hours. Jim wanted to start at midnight, and be entirely done by 4 p.m.; Dave wanted to be free between 10 a.m. and 4 p.m.; Peter wanted to relieve Dave after his second shift; Mike, finally, had to be on duty at 9 a.m.

What shift pattern did they finally settle on?

SOLUTION ON PAGE 135

DAVEY

Wiggins had finished describing his latest discoveries to us, and rather than take off, he hung around to share an anecdote. "A funny thing happened to me on the South Bank this morning, Mr Holmes."

"Is that so?"

"On my honour," Wiggins said, with an impish grin. "I was almost up to opposite the Palace of Westminster when I happened to glance over my shoulder, and saw my old pal Davey heading in my direction, about 200 yards away. So I turned around, and headed towards him. Two hundred yards of facing each other later, him grinning at me every step we took, he was still 200 yards away. Can you credit it?"

"Very rum," Holmes said, allowing himself a small smile.

He had to explain it to me, but can you see what had happened?

SOLUTION ON PAGE 135

LOOSE CHANGE

It occurs to me that an experience of my own may prove a worthy addition to this collection of problems. When I returned home to 221b from the trip to Hookland, I found myself rather short on ready money. I had kept receipts and other notes, so I had a solid idea of where it had all gone.

At the start of the journey, my ticket from Hookland back to London cost me precisely one half of the money I had available. Before boarding, I also bought a fortifying mug of tea for Holmes and myself, at a cost of sixpence. When we arrived back in London, it was lunchtime, so I treated the pair of us to a pub lunch at Waterloo, which cost me half of what I had remaining, plus ten further pence to boot. Half of what that left me went on getting back across town to Paddington. Then I gave sixpence to an old beggar outside the station, and paid nine pence for a quick shoe-shine. When I got home, I discovered that I had just one solitary sixpence left.

How much did I start out with? Feel free to calculate the sum in pennies.

SOLUTION ON PAGE 136

THE FIFTH WORDKNOT

I received my fifth wordknot from Holmes over a rather nice luncheon at the Great Western Hotel at Paddington, a fine example of mid-century Second Empire architecture and design, with lavish ornamentation. The hotel, that is, rather than the luncheon, which was nevertheless quite outstanding.

I did my best to address Holmes' challenge adroitly, but I must confess that the goose was quite a distraction. The note he gave me is replicated below, and the task, as I'm sure you recall, is to unpick the three ten-letter words whose letters are scrambled in the ten rows below, first letters on the first row, second letters on the second row, and so on. The words are of course thematically related.

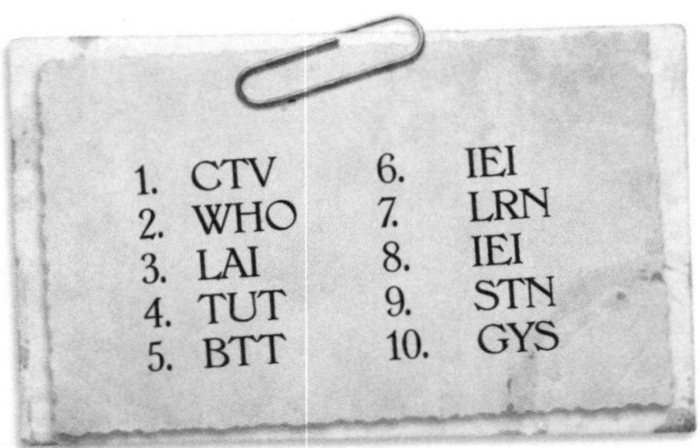

1. CTV
2. WHO
3. LAI
4. TUT
5. BTT
6. IEI
7. LRN
8. IEI
9. STN
10. GYS

SOLUTION ON PAGE 136

THE LEASE

Mrs Hudson was cleaning away our breakfast things. "That Archie, he does think he's a wit. Well, he's half-right."

"Archie?" I asked, in a moment of incaution.

"A cousin, on Mr Hudson's side," she said.

I breathed a sigh of relief. "How many cousins do you actually have, Mrs Hudson?" I couldn't help myself.

"Seventy-nine," she told me. "No, make that 78. That fool Neill died last month. Fell off a cliff. There's only 22 as I'd consider top shelf, though. Anyway, I was telling you about Archie."

"Indeed you were," I admitted.

"Well, Archie lives in a small place up Wembley way. He's on a 99-year lease, and I thought to ask him how much time there was left on it. So he only tells me, all smug like, that two-thirds of the time that's expired is equal to four-fifths of the time remaining. Of course, a gentleman like yourself wouldn't be fazed by that for an instant, would you?"

"Of course not," I managed. Holmes snickered from across the room.

How long is left on the lease?

SOLUTION ON PAGE 137

TEA

Holmes turned to look at me, fixing me with his gaze until I lowered my book. "Have you ever considered the plight of the humble grocer, Watson?"

I admitted that I had not, in general, spent a great deal of time attempting to evaluate the life of grocers, no.

"Scales can be a positively devilish business," he said.

"Is that so?"

"Most definitely. Imagine that you are such a grocer, in urgent need of dividing a 20-pound bale of tea into two-pound packets. The only weights you have to use on your scale are one weighing nine pounds, and one weighing five pounds. What would be the least number of weighings you would need to divide up your bale correctly?"

What do you think?

SOLUTION ON PAGE 138

The Seamstress

During *The Adventure of the Impossible Gecko*, we interviewed a seamstress who'd seen a suspicious man loitering around outside her employers' manor house in rural Essex. The house was robbed a day later, and a priceless jewel-studded jade gecko – which really ought not to have existed, given all historical precedent – went missing. Naturally, the Turners recalled the information that the seamstress had passed to them the night before, so it was a clear necessity that we interview her.

When she arrived at 221b Baker Street, Miss Adams seemed polite and pleasant, if somewhat over-awed. Holmes looked her over, and spotted several sure signs of her profession, including needle-spotting on the second joint of her thumb, and a very specific callus on her index finger. Comfortable with her bona fides, he interviewed her.

We learnt from Miss Adams that it was a drizzly night when she saw the man out on the grounds, observing the house. She was working in a room on the ground floor, and caught sight of him near the tree-line, some 40 feet away. Although she was unable to see the man's face, she said that he was around six feet in height, and strongly built. He watched the house for several minutes, before turning around and slinking away. She immediately went to inform the Turners.

As soon as she left the building, Holmes leapt to his feet, grabbed a tattered coat from a closet, and dashed after her. All he'd spare me by way of explanation was that she was clearly lying. Can you say why?

SOLUTION ON PAGE 139

ODD

Holmes was clutching some sort of disturbingly decorated thuribile, and holding forth on the vital necessity of allowing one's mind to think outside of the rigidly inflexible train-tracks of conventional thought. The thurible, which had come from an abandoned church, was glittering in the sunlight as he waved it around the drawing-room. It kept drawing my eye, to my annoyance, as the peculiar script with which it was engraved made me feel more than a little uneasy.

"The superior mind must not be blinkered, Watson. Watson?"

"Ah, yes, Holmes. Not blinkered. Quite so."

"I'm glad you agree," he said, tossing the glittering censer from one hand to the other and back. "So. Write down five odd digits for me that will add up to 14."

I paused at that. "An odd number of odd numbers coming up even? That's impossible, surely?"

Holmes sighed. "What was I just saying?"

Can you find a solution?

SOLUTION ON PAGE 140

SPEED

Speed was something of an issue to the Baker Street Irregulars. When one lives as a street urchin, a swift pair of heels is an extremely important quality. So the Irregulars often engaged in competitive sprints – not so much for status, but to ascertain whose skills were more suited to which types of endeavour.

On one afternoon, Wiggins told us about some of that morning's races. The fastest member of the Irregulars was a 12-year-old named Sid, who'd somehow found his way to London from Newcastle upon Tyne. He'd been putting a new recruit, named Raymond, to the test. In a series of 100-yard sprints, Sid had consistently beaten Ray by ten yards. Having seen Sid run, I was duly impressed by Ray's performance.

"At the end, after their rest break, Ray wanted one fair crack," Wiggins said. "So he asked Sid to start ten yards behind the line." He and Holmes both chuckled.

"I'm sure you can see what the outcome was, old chap," Holmes said to me. I snapped off an answer, and immediately regretted it. Can you find the solution?

SOLUTION ON PAGE

141

Bees

"It's interesting," Holmes said, "the lengths to which people will go in order to obfuscate perfectly simple information."

"Imagine that," I said.

"Well, Watson, you of all people should be highly familiar with such manipulations." I must have looked slightly dismayed at that, for he followed up swiftly. "Having spent so much time exposed to academic research during your medical training."

"Ah. Yes, that. Damnable stuff, Holmes. Self-aggrandizement at its worst, often."

"Precisely." Holmes nodded. "Take this, which comes from a letter I received from an apiarist I have been corresponding with in Devon. He says, of a small hive, that one-fifth of the workers typically went to his azaleas, one-third to his roses, and a number equal to three times the difference between these two fractions to his geraniums, leaving the remaining worker to dart about uncertainly."

"Does he now?" I asked. "I suppose you'd like me to tell you how many worker bees there were in total?"

"Excellent, Watson. Indeed I would."

Any idea?

FRUITFUL

Holmes had been downstairs to have a word with Mrs Hudson regarding cabbage, and returned carrying a large orange.

"Did you settle the cabbage matter to your satisfaction, old chap?" I asked him.

"Quite so," he replied. "That woman is a fountain of information."

"Indeed she is," I agreed, thinking of her frequent tales of her bewildering assortment of relatives and their in-laws.

"Did you know that she keeps a bowl of fruit downstairs?"

"Of course," I said.

"There's a number of pieces of fruit in there today. Given my depredations, all but two of them are oranges, all but two of them are pears, and all but two of them are apples. How many is that?"

Can you find the solution?

SOLUTION ON PAGE 142

The Third Camouflage

I was returning home from a shopping trip, carrying several quite sizeable bags, when Holmes accosted me on the street just outside the door to 221b. "Wait, Watson. Do not enter!"

I flinched slightly, surprised at his appearance, and stopped where I was.

"Tourbillion," barked Holmes. "Underfunded. Candyfloss. Tessellated."

After my initial panicked moment, where I feared the poor fellow had suffered a major stroke, I realized that he was assigning me one of his camouflage puzzles. Four words, each containing a smaller word, such that the smaller words are thematically linked. I confess that my relief at his ongoing wellbeing quite drove the words from my mind, and it was rather a fight to retrieve them.

What was the uniting theme?

SOLUTION ON PAGE 142

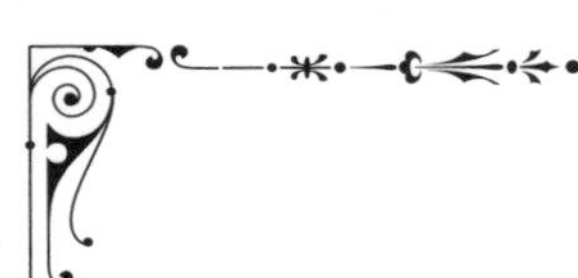

DRAUGHT

March was approaching slowly, and the weather outside was frightful. Snow, snow and more snow had been piling up for days, and despite the well-heaped fireplace, 221b was decidedly chilly. Holmes was standing by the window, gazing out onto the street, and making quiet deductions to himself about passing strangers, as was his occasional habit. Then he turned to face me.

"You'll have noticed that there's a cold draught coming from the window, my dear friend."

"I have indeed," I said.

"I can assure you that the window is perfectly sound, mechanically. There is no gap or chink in either glass or woodwork. So where's the draught coming from?"

That floored me for a bit. What do you think?

SOLUTION ON PAGE 143

RUDIMENTARY

ANSWERS AND SOLUTIONS

"Any truth is better than indefinite doubt."

Sherlock Holmes

ON THE STRAND

The teacher and the tailor were both women, and therefore vanishingly unlikely to be named Hugo.

GRANDDAD

As Holmes has often said, “Once you eliminate the impossible, whatever remains, no matter how improbable, must be the truth.” The highwayman married late in life, and the grandfather in question was her mother’s father, not her father’s father.

SPHERES

Three points on a sphere will always be able to be encompassed by one hemisphere. If you visualize two points on the boundary of one hemisphere and the third tipping over an edge into the other, it should be immediately obvious that all three then fall within the reverse of that first hemisphere. Once you escape the idea that the hemispheres are fixed in some pre-decided pattern, the matter is very simple. Being a certainty of course, the probability is 1.

HOOKLAND

The minimum number to meet those conditions would be seven moles – three of them totally blind, two blind in the right eye, one blind in the left eye, and one with normal vision. You'll note that seven left eyes (four blind, three sighted) and seven right eyes (five blind, two sighted) are specifically mentioned. The maximum, of course, would be 15: 5 + 4 + 3 + 2 + 1.

THE WATCHMEN

As it turned out, it was rather obvious, yes. Picture the route as a circle, and imagine the guards setting off both clockwise and anti-clockwise simultaneously. There inevitably comes a moment where the two guards will meet. That is the time (and place) where the guard will have to be every hour, whichever way he is walking.

THE PRISON

Since you can make any number between 00000 and 99999, and no others, there are precisely 100,000 possible combinations for the lock.

THE FIRST WORDKNOT

The words are *chocolates, delicacies* and *peppermint.*

WHISKY

Seven shillings is 84p. If the whisky is worth 80 pence more than the glass, and the glass is worth x, then (80 + x) is the value of the whisky, and x + 80 + x = 84. So the glass is worth tuppence, or two pence.

COUSIN TRACY

Three. As both Tracy and Albert have six children, and the children of their marriage must be counted for both of them, they must have had the same number of children before they were married. There are only four possibilities, from one child together and five each separately (a total of 11) to five children together, and one each separately (a total of seven). We know the total is nine children, so both Tracy and Albert had three children each before marrying, and then three more together.

THE CANDLES

There are lots of numbers that are difficult to get to, but 100 can be achieved with two boxes of 16 candles, and four boxes of 17.

PASSING BY

The two trains running in opposite directions go 400 + 200 = 600ft (relative to each other) in five seconds, a total relative speed of 600/5 = 120ft/s. If running in the same direction, they would travel the same relative distance in 15 seconds, at a total speed of 600/15 = 40ft/s. So x + y = 120, and x – y = 40. As x – y = 40, x = 40 + y, so y + 40 + y = 120, or 2y = 80. Thus y = 80/2, or 40. So then x + 40 = 120, and x = 80. As 80 is greater than 40, the faster train is moving at 80ft/s – which, incidentally, is 54.54 miles per hour, as 1 f/s is approximately 0.682 mph. Do note that you'd have had to receive further information to be able to say which train was the faster (it was the shorter, if you're curious).

TRILOGY

If the former officer died without regaining consciousness, there is no way anyone could know what he had been dreaming about. The story has to be a fabrication.

BUCKETS

The weights would be identical. An object floating in water displaces an amount of water such that the weight of the water displaced is precisely equal to the weight of the object.

THE MADDENED MILLER

One ninth of a bushel. If the miller took a tenth, then one bushel must be 9/10ths of the flour, so the original volume would have been 1 * 10/9 bushels, or 1 and 1/9th.

THE PAINTING

The price drops to 5/8ths of its previous amount each time. I purchased it for 25/64ths of £250, which to the nearest pound is £98 – £97.65625, to be exact.

THE FIRST CAMOUFLAGE

The words are *ant*, *bee*, *bug* and *moth*, and they are all types of insect.

FABULOUS

22. The arrogant runner (A) has travelled 1/6th of the course. During the time he has been running, his opponent has run 5/6ths – 1/8th of the course (because of his head-start). Convert that to 24ths, and A has gone 4/24ths while B has gone 17/24ths. We can drop the divisors to say that A runs four while B runs 17, so B is moving 17/4 times faster than A. A has five times as far to go, however. So, to just tie with B, A would need to run at (17/4)*5 times his original speed, or 21.25 times. So, to win, rounding to the nearest whole number, A would need to go 22 times as fast as he had been going.

OUT EAST

60 per cent. The same number of men and women must have been married, so whatever number that is, it represents 2.1 per cent of men and 1.4 per cent of women. Simplifying those numbers, we see that the ratio of male to female inhabitants must be 2:3. So 3/5ths of the population – 60 per cent – are female.

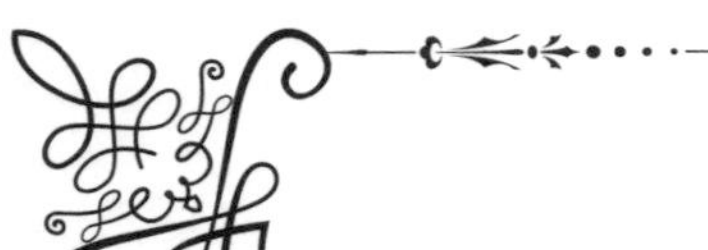

THE SUICIDE

There was no source of liquid anywhere in the room. Whilst not strictly impossible that our client's uncle had forced himself to dry-swallow a score of large pills, it did seem an unlikely inconvenience to inflict on oneself during one's last moments. In fact, he'd been poisoned, and although the killer staged the pills and removed the poisoned beverage, he totally forgot to replace the latter.

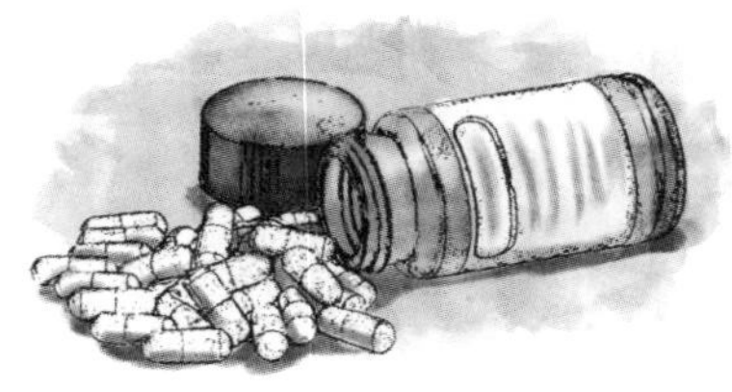

SCARVES

0. It's impossible. If 11 of the scarves have gone to their correct owners, then the twelfth must also have gone to its own owner too. There's no one else for it to go to.

JOE

Joe is ten and Ruth is four. The only time when relative ages move so swiftly is when one of the people is very young. If you try one as Ruth's initial age, you'll quickly see that all the ratios pan out – one and seven, two and eight, and three and nine, which makes them currently four and ten.

THE WENNS

33. Since there are more patrons than numbers of pennies, and no sum of pennies can be duplicated, the number of pennies each patron has must be represented by a continuous arithmetical distribution of rising 0, 1, 2, 3, etc. With both duplicate amounts and 33 pennies being forbidden, a theoretical 34th patron would have no possible number of pennies to be allocated. So the most people that there can be is if there are 33 patrons ranging from 0 to 32 pennies.

MAIDA VALE

Ten miles. James is going twice as fast as Gerry, and so will catch up to him in one hour, at the four-mile point. The dog is thus running at ten miles per hour, continually, for one hour.

SHEEP

960. David gets 1,200 sheep, as 200 is 20 per cent of 1000. Now, x + 25% = 5x/4, so to find x, we must divide by 5/4, or multiple by 4/5, which is 0.8. As 1,200 * 0.8 = 960, Caradog gets 960 sheep.

THE SECOND WORDKNOT

The words are *tourmaline*, *aquamarine* and *rhodolites.*

THE PARTNER

£800 to Gerry, and £200 to James. If a third of the business is £1,000, then the whole business must have been worth £3,000. Of this, 60 per cent belongs to Gerry, and 40 per cent to James. After the deal, both James and Gerry will own 33.3 per cent of the business, so James is losing 6.6 per cent while Gerry is losing 26.6 per cent. Expressing those lost percentages in thirds for simplicity will give us James's loss at 20/3, and Gerry's at 80/3. So the money should be shared between James and Gerry in the ratio 20:80. Thus James should get £200, and Gerry £800.

FRUITY

7. The pear = 1 apple + 6 plums. We know that 3 apples + 1 pear = 10 plums, so replacing the pear with 1 apple + 6 plums, we get 4 apple + 6 plums = 10 plums. That means apples and plums have the same weight. We know that the pear = 1 apple + 6 plums, so since 1 apple = 1 plum, the pear weighs 7 plums.

CIDER

7,890. 146 + 31 = 177. Dividing that into equal length and width (and remembering that one tree serves double duty at the corner) gives us a square of 89 * 89 trees. But this is the extended size of the plot, so the currently planted trees are 88 * 88 in number, or 7,744.

HANDS

It will be even. Two people are required for a handshake, so the total number of people shaking hands from any subset of total handshakes must always be even.

A SENSE OF URGENCY

Anything multiplied by 0 is 0.

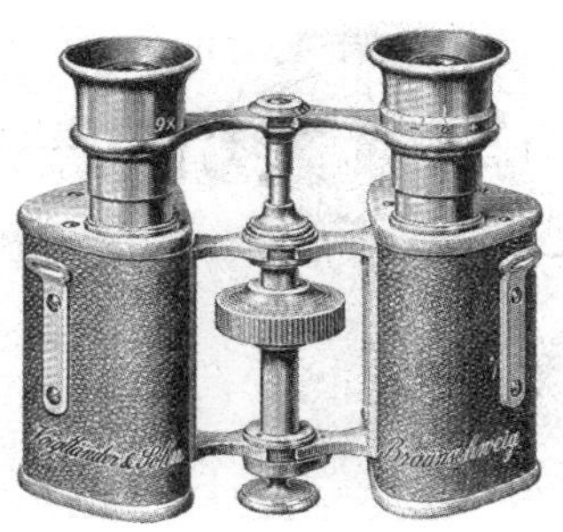

HOT AND COLD

Hot air rises, so we warm things above heat sources. Cold air thus of necessity sinks. Your best option is to place the ice on top of the cube, where it can cool your metal both with physical contact, and with the cold air flowing down from the ice.

ON THE BUSES

18 miles. Smith's walking speed is a third of his riding speed, so he spends 75 per cent of the time walking. 75 per cent of eight hours is six hours, and 6 x 3 = 18.

HOOKLAND KNIGHTS

The number 16 belongs with the second knight. On the first knight, the pairs of numbers are all made up in their entirety of curved lines. On the second knight, the pairs of numbers contain both curved and straight lines. On the third knight, the numbers are entirely made up of straight lines.

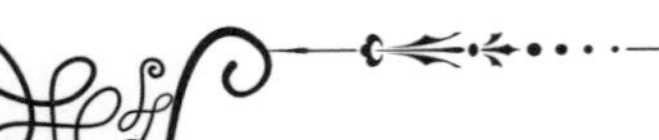

THE THIRD WORDKNOT

The words are acrobatics, daredevils, and tightropes.

DANIEL

The corpse is on top of the rope coils. Boutros was at the bottom of the rope, and since we know he was being belayed from above, the rest of the rope was above him. Wherever the rope fell, if it had snapped – or even been let go – the rope would be next to or above the body, not beneath it. Dickey must have thrown Boutros off the top of the cliff, after one of the two of them sent the rope over (whether deliberately or accidentally).

ANSWERS AND SOLUTIONS

"As a rule, the most bizarre a thing is, the less mysterious it proves to be."

Sherlock Holmes

THE PLEASANT LAKE

The missing letter is "E", and the inscription says "Persevere, ye perfect men; Ever keep these precepts ten".

THE UNCLE

He's 60. Those fractional amounts work out to 12/60ths as a child, 15/60ths as a youth and 20/60ths as a man.
12 + 15 + 20 = 47. 60 – 47 = 13. So 13/60ths of x, his total age = 13 years, and in turn, x = 13 * 60 / 13, which is trivially 60.

SLICK

It transpires that ice is not actually slippery, no more than stone is. However, its melting point is dependent on pressure. When you put weight on it, it melts (provided that the temperature is not way below freezing), and it is the water that is slippery. It refreezes when you move on. When you walk on rough ice, you have fewer points of contact between ice and shoe, and so your weight is concentrated, increasing the pressure, the amount of water, and the slipperiness. Walking on very smooth ice spreads your weight out, and minimizes the melting.

THE SECOND CAMOUFLAGE

The words are *ear*, *eye*, *lip* and *nose*, and they are all parts of the face.

FORTY-FIVE

One of the numbers has to be a quarter of one of the others, so the larger must be divisible by 4. Together, these two must add to a little more than the sum of the other two numbers, so the largest must be a small amount less than half our target. 24 and 6 both give us 12 when operated on according to instructions, but would mean the other two had to be 14 and 10, which do not sum to 15. But 20 and 5 both give 10 when adjusted, and 45 – 25 = 20, which fits with 8 and 12. So the numbers are 8, 12, 5 and 20, and 8 + 2 = 12 – 2 = 5*2 = 20/2 = 10.

ST MARY AXE

7.5 miles. As Lloyd spends part of the time at 5 mph and part at 3 mph, the time he spends at each speed must be in the ration 3:5. So three hours at 5 mph = five hours at 3 mph = 15 miles. But that journey would take eight hours, not four, so the distance is half of 15 miles.

GREAT-AUNT ADA

There are only a few pairs of digits which give a gap of 45 depending on how they're ordered. So the ages could be 05 & 50, 16 & 61, 27 & 72, 38 & 83, and 49 & 94. Of these options, the only pair of primes are 2 and 7. So Ada would be 72, making Mrs Hudson a most unlikely 27 – I can see why Holmes snorted.

RONNIE

£556. Where x is the cloak's value, x + 500 = 12 (months), and x + 60 = 7. Combining those, we can say that x + 60 = 7*(x + 500)/12. Thus 12x + 720 = 7x + 3500, so 5x = 2780, and x = 556. A modest year's salary does seem rather a staggering amount for a cape, unless it was a hand-me-down from Good Queen Bess herself, or made from overlapping scales of solid gold.

FEBRUARY

1928. There are only five of anything in February during a leap year, and then only one day, so it follows that each day of the week must get a fifth February appearance every 28 years. However, centuries are only a leap year if they are divisible by four, which rules 1900 out. The next five-Wednesday February after 1888 thus has to be 1928.

THE CODE

Since you know the word is English, the simplest way of finding it is a matter of discovering the one-word anagrams of GAUNTOILER. The only one in common usage is REGULATION. If you prefer to attack the matter mathematically, consider the position of the numbers in the sum given. With two five-figure numbers adding to a six-figure one, the first digit of the answer, R, can only be "1". For the start of the five-digit numbers, we see that G + O leave G in the units again. If either G or O was 0, the answer would be five-digit not six, so there must be 1 carrying over from the next column along, and O must be "9". Similarly, A + I >= 10, in order to give the number to carry over. At the end, we see T + R = I, but R is 1, so we know I must be one greater than T. N + E = E means N must be 0. U + L must equal 9. I don't have the room here, but keep pressing the matter on this basis, and the puzzle will fall. The sum, incidentally, is 36,407 + 98,521 = 134,928.

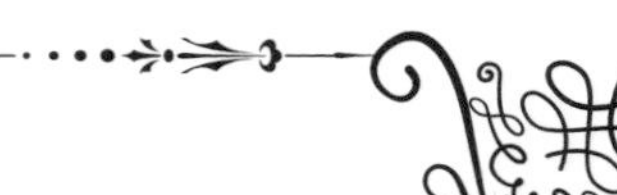

ISAAC

The trick is to obtain a pair of objects that will present an identical profile to the air, but which you can contrive to give different weight to. You then drop them, and observe them falling simultaneously. We settled on a pair of matchboxes, one with matches in and one filled with coins, but there's no end of possibilities. A pair of bottles, one empty and one full, dropped onto a cushion, perhaps.

THE TRACK

9 minutes 20 seconds. Blue is moving 4/7 the speed of red, and red needs to have run blue's distance plus one whole lap in order to pass him. After one lap of red's, blue is 3/7 of a lap behind. After two, he's 6/7 down. It should be obvious that red is closing the distance at exactly 3/7ths of a lap for each lap of his own. He has 1/7th to go, so that will take him a third of a lap. So the total distance is 2 and 1/3rd laps, which at 4 minutes a lap is 9 minutes and 20 seconds.

A CHELSEA TALE

It turned out that Jez (short for Jeremy, apparently) is a window-cleaner. He was on the outside of the building, and when he panicked, he jumped into the room in front of him.

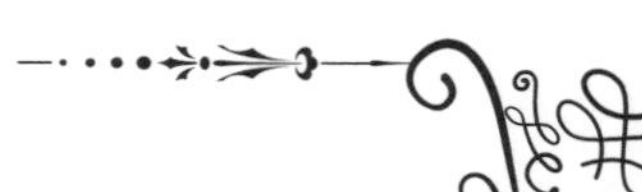

EXPRESS

Although I was right about the impending question, it proved not to be algebraic so much as logical. If the trains are running at 60 mph and 40 mph, then an hour ago, they were 60 + 40 = 100 miles apart.

THE FENCE

If the length of the fence is y feet, and the number of posts is x, then x + 150 = y = 3(x – 70) = 3x – 210. So we can say that 2x = 360, or x = 180 (and, by the by, y = which would give an area of around 6,806 sq ft if made into a square enclosure, or, maximally, an area of 8,666 sq ft as a circular area of radius 52.52ft).

THE FOURTH WORDKNOT

The words are *underscore*, *subheading* and *typesetter*.

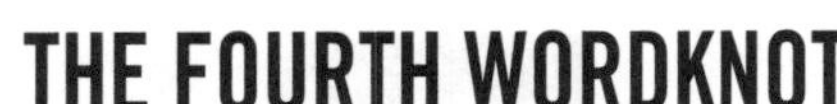

THE ONE

It is comprised of all ten digits in English alphabetical order.

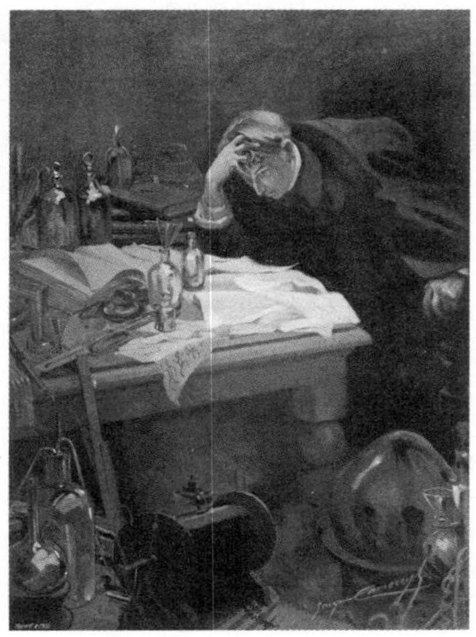

BISCUITS

It was Stephen. Only one of the statements is true. Since Will and Stephen's statements are mutually exclusive, the true statement must be one of them. Now, assume Stephen's statement is true, and he is innocent. In this instance, the opposites of the other statements do not give a definite solution – it could still be either Mary or Gwen, neither of whom are wrongfully accused (and thus given an alibi when their accusations are negated). Since Wiggins had an immediate solution, the statements must give a firm answer. Thus Will is telling the truth, and Stephen stole (and ate) the biscuits.

DANGEROUS LADIES

AD 30. Since the ladies had a total lifespan of 69 years over the course of 129 years, there must have been 60 years when neither were alive. So Boadicea was born 60 years after 30 BC – in AD 30.

SQUARE SHEEP

12. What I finally remembered is that a circle is the most perfectly compact expression of any given area, so it follows that for any given perimeter length – i.e., number of matches – the closer your shape gets to a circle, the bigger the area it contains. In this instance, a perfectly regular 12-sided shape (a dodecagon) with sides of length 1 will give you an area of 11.19y2, since the area of a dodecagon is 0.5 * 12 * side-length * distance from centre to the middle of any side (which is 1.865 * side-length). Similarly, a perfectly regular 11-sided shape (an endecagon) with sides of length 1 works out at 9.365y2. So you can make a 10y2 space with 12 yard-long fences.

MR ANDREAS

£14,315. To calculate simple compound interest of this sort (that is, where the interest is calculated once per designated time unit), you can calculate the 55 per cent manually, add it to the base sum, and repeat a series of times. But it is simpler and more efficient to use the formula A = P * (1+r)^t, where A is the accrued wealth, P is the principal (or initial) capital, r is the rate of interest as a fraction, and t is the number of iterations. So in this instance, A = 1600 * (1+0.55)^5, or 1600 * 8.9466.

THE BOTTLE

You need three measurements. First of all, measure the diameter of the base, and use that to find the area of the base. Then stand the bottle upright, and measure the height of the liquid from the base. Finally, turn the bottle upside down, and measure the height of the empty space from the top of the liquid (which will be well above the start of the neck) to the base. You now have measurements for the volume filled by liquid – the area of the base * the height of the liquid – and the volume filled by air, area of base * height of air. As there is nothing else in there, add these two together to find the volume of the bottle.

HOW MANY COWS?

121,393. The Fibonacci sequence is a famous mathematical model describing exponential growth of precisely this kind, such that each number in the sequence is the sum of the two numbers preceding it. It runs 0, 1, 1, 2, 3, 5, 8, ..., where in this instance, the terms of the sequence would indicate the number of calves produced in that year. It is useful here to note that the sum total of all numbers up to any Nth term in the sequence is equal to the (N+2)th term minus one. Further more, as N = (N–1) + (N–2) – the basic definition of the sequence – then also (N+2) = 2*(N) + (N–1). So from those two, it follows that if we know two sequential terms, N and N–1, then the total of all the values in the sequence up to N is equal to 2*(N) + (N–1) –1. The 24th and 25th terms of the sequence are 48,368 and 28,657, so the black woodland cow would have a total of 2*(48,368)+(28,657)–1=121,392 descendants in that time. She, of course, is still active, for a total 121,393 cows. That's a lot of cows behaving quite oddly, so I can see Mr Podge's concern somewhat.

THE WATCH

Jim worked 00:00 – 06:00 and 10:00 – 16:00.

Dave worked 04:00 – 10:00 and 16:00 – 22:00.

Peter worked 12:00 – 18:00 and 22:00 – 04:00.

Mike worked 06:00 – 12:00 and 18:00 – 00:00.

DAVEY

The only possible answer is that when Wiggins turned around and started walking towards Davey, Davey started walking backwards at the same pace. Peculiar behaviour, to be sure.

LOOSE CHANGE

I started out with 220p, which is of course just tuppence short of 19 shillings. The trick is to start at the end and work backwards. So 6 + 9 + 6 = 21*2 = 42 + 10 = 52*2 = 104 + 6 = 110*2 = 220.

THE FIFTH WORDKNOT

Twittering. Chattiness. Volubility.

THE LEASE

45. From Archie's statement, $4x/5 = 2y/3$, and $x + y = 99$. So $12x = 10y$, or $x = 10y/12$. Now substitute, so $10y/12 + y = 99$, or $10y + 12y = 1188$, or $22y = 1188$, so $y = 54$. Then, $x + 54 = 99$, or $x = 45$. There are 45 years left.

TEA

9. First, place the 5lb and 9lb weights in different pans, so that 4lb of tea will balance them. Weigh four such 4lb lots, leaving (of necessity) 4lbs in the bale. Then take each 4lb lot in turn, remove the weights from the scales, and divide each lot so that it is perfectly balanced. This will add five weighings to the four previous, for a total of nine.

THE SEAMSTRESS

When it's dark, it's very hard to see anything outside from a lit room. This is particularly true when it's raining, no matter how lightly. Since the house is in a rural environment, there would have been nothing in the way of extra light to illuminate the fellow. She must have made up the intruder to prepare the way for some other mischief to take place.

ODD

My eventual answer was to combine two 1s to make 11, so that 11 + 1 + 1 + 1 = 14. You could do it other ways if you added in other mathematical operations – 1/1 + 9 + 3 + 1, for example.

SPEED

Sid won again. In the previous races, Ray ran 90y whilst Sid ran 100y. So in the last race, Ray and Sid would be neck and neck at the 90-yard point, Ray having run 90y and Sid 100y. In the remaining 10y, Sid continued outpacing Ray and won.

BEES

Just 15 bees, which seems to me to be a low estimate by a factor of 1,000, even for a small hive. Still, we must tackle the situation as expressed by Holmes' correspondent. We know that two of the factions of bees represent 1/5th and 1/3rd of the workers. Expressing those figures in a common denominator makes for 3/15ths and 5/15ths. The difference between these amounts is 2/15ths, which multiplied by three gives us 6/15ths. These bees account for 3 + 5 + 6 = 14/15ths of the workers. The remaining 1/15th of the workers is one bee, so 1*15 = 15.

FRUITFUL

It is just three pieces of fruit, one of each type, as a moment's thought will swiftly make clear.

THE THIRD CAMOUFLAGE

The words were *bill*, *fund*, *loss* and *sell*, and the theme was business.

DRAUGHT

As the window cools, the air in the room next to it gets colder. Cold air sinks, so the warmer air of the room gets pulled down to fill the space. Then it too chills. This effect produces a circular draught from fireplace to window, with warm air running along the ceiling, and cold air along the floor. We feel this as a draught. This is part of the reason why Mr San Galli's excellent heating radiators are often placed below windows.

Also Available

Sherlock Holmes' Elementary Puzzles
978-1-78097-578-8

Sherlock Holmes' Fiendish Puzzles
978-1-78097-807-9

Sherlock Holmes' Cunning Puzzles
978-1-78097-962-5